Fre

de

ric Masson

# An Account of Three Journeys from the Cape Town into the Southern Parts of Africa

Undertaken for the Discovery of New Plants, towards the Improvement of the Royal Botanical Gardens at Kew. By Mr. Francis Masson, One of His Majesty's Gardeners.

Fre

de

ric Masson

**An Account of Three Journeys from the Cape Town into the Southern Parts of Africa**

*Undertaken for the Discovery of New Plants, towards the Improvement of the Royal Botanical Gardens at Kew. By Mr. Francis Masson, One of His Majesty's Gardeners.*

ISBN/EAN: 9783337213473

Printed in Europe, USA, Canada, Australia, Japan

Cover: Foto ©Andreas Hilbeck / pixelio.de

More available books at **www.hansebooks.com**

XVI. *An Account of Three Journeys from the* Cape Town *into the Southern Parts of* Africa; *undertaken for the Difcovery of new Plants, towards the Improvement of the Royal Botanical Gardens at* Kew. *By Mr.* Francis Maffon, *one of his Majefty's Gardeners. Addreffed to Sir* John Pringle, *Bart. P. R. S.*

### TO SIR JOHN PRINGLE, BART. P. R. S.

S I R,                                         Kew, Nov. 1775.

R. Feb. 1,
1776.
IN compliance with your requeft, I now fend you the account of my firft journey from the Cape, which I have tranfcribed from my journal; and if you fhall find it to contain any thing worthy the notice of the Royal Society, I beg you would do me the honour to prefent it to that illuftrious Body; and believe, that with the greateft pleafure I fhall communicate to you and to them the remaining part of my obfervations.

I am, &c.

A N

## AN ACCOUNT OF THE FIRST JOURNEY.

ON the 10th of December, 1772, I set out from the Cape Town, towards the evening, attended by a Dutchman, and a Hottentot who drove my waggon, which was drawn by eight oxen; this being the manner of travelling there. They prefer oxen to horses, because they are much cheaper, and more easily maintained. At sun-set we crossed the Salt River, about two miles distance from the Cape Town, where is placed a high flag-staff with a large old piece of cannon, intended to give signals to prevent a surprize from an enemy: these signals are answered by others, placed upon eminences at proper distances, and alarm the adjacent country in a short time. In the night we travelled over a large sandy plain; and towards the morning stopped at a small cottage called Elsis Kraal. The next day we partook of the diversion of hunting a small species of antelope, which the Dutch call Steenbock. We crossed great part of this sandy plain, which is very extensive, reaching from the Tyger Berg to Bay Falso, upwards of twenty miles; from the Table Mountain to Hottentot Holland Mountains, about thirty miles. The soil of this plain is unfit for cultivation; being a pure white sand, blown by the S.E. wind from the shore of Falso Bay, and often forming large hillocks; it is, nevertheless, overgrown with an infinite variety of plants peculiar to this country.

7

11th, We paſſed the Tyger Berg, leaving it on our left hand; and along its ſkirts ſaw many fine plantations, abounding with corn fields and vineyards.

12th, We paſſed the Paerden Berg (that is, Horſes Mountain) ſo called from the number of Zebras formerly found there, which are called by the Dutch inhabitants wild horſes. Towards the evening, croſſing the Berg Rivier (that is, Mountain River) we entered into the diſtrict called Draakenſteen, a valley about ten miles in length, and about five in breadth; containing many large plantations of vineyards, and orchards of moſt kinds of European fruit, which have been tranſported hither by the Dutch; *viz.* apricots, peaches, plumbs, apples, pears, figs, mulberries, almonds, cheſnuts, and walnuts; but no Indian fruits, except the guyava and jambo, neither of which ripen well.      Theſe plantations are generally ſituated near the foot of the mountains, and watered by ſmall ſtreams, which deſcend with great rapidity, and are conveyed all over their gardens and vineyards.

16th, We travelled to a ſmall village called Perel, ſo named from its ſituation on the N.E. ſide of a hill called Perel Berg. In it is a church and about a dozen of houſes diſperſed along the foot of the hill, with pretty gardéns and vineyards, which produce excellent wine.

17th, I went up to the top of the Perel Berg, where I ſpent a whole day in ſearch of plants, and hunting a ſort of antelope called Ree Bock; but had no ſucceſs.      I ſaw nothing here ſo worthy of obſervation as two large ſolid rocks, of a roundiſh figure; each of which, I may poſi-
tively

tively fay, is more than a mile about at the bafe, and upwards of two hundred feet high above the ground. Their furfaces are nearly fmooth, without chink or fiffures, and they are found to be a fpecies of *faxum* or granite, different from that which compofe the neighbouring mountains.

18th, From hence we continued our journey to a valley, adjoining the S. E. part of Draakenfteen, called Franfche Hoek[a]; it having been fettled by a party of French refugees, who left France about the beginning of this century. Though but a poor fettlement, being a cold, moorifh foil, it produces corn enough for its inhabitants, four wine and fome fruit. Drakenfteen and Franfche Hoek are bounded on the N.E. and S.E. by a chain of high mountains, which have their beginning at Cape Falfo, run in a winding courfe to the N.W. of St. Helena Bay, and fend out feveral branches into the interior parts of the country. Thefe two vallies are watered by the Berg Rivier, which rifes in the Stellenbofch mountains. It is a confiderable river, but no where navigable. The banks are decorated with a great variety of uncommon trees.

January 4, 1773, We reached Stellenbofch, a fmall village about thirty miles N.E. from the Cape Town, confifting of about thirty houfes, forming one regular ftreet, with a row of large oak-trees on each fide along the front of the houfes, which render it very pleafant in

(a) This, I fuppofe, to be the place which fome of the French voyagers in their obfervations on the Cape of Good Hope, call Petite Rochelle.

the

the hot feafon. Thefe oaks, which are of the fame fort with ours in England, were brought out of Europe by ADRIAN VANDERSTELL, formerly governor of the Cape, who built this village, and gave it his name. The country round it is populous, and contains many rich farms, which produce plenty of corn and wine. It is watered by a fmall river called Eerfte Rivier, which difcharges itfelf into the Eaft part of Falfo Bay. The farmers we found bufy in treading out their corn; which is performed by horfes in the following manner. They make a circular floor about thirty, forty, or fifty feet diameter, with a compofition of clay and cow-dung, which binds very hard; round it they erect a mud wall, about breaft high; this floor they cover with fheaves, beginning in the middle, and laying them in concentric circles till they reach the outfide. They then turn in about twenty or thirty horfes, which a Hottentot, furnifhed with a long whip, drives round and round till the corn be trodden out, and the ftraw become as fine as chaff; which they afterwards clean, and carry into their granaries. This method they can practice with great fecurity, as it feldom rains here from the middle of October to the middle of March.

5th, From thence we travelled along the foot of the Stellenbofch mountains to Hottentot Holland, a pleafant and level country; furrounded on three fides by the mountains; and the other opening to the Eaft part of Falzo Bay. In it are eight or ten plantations, with elegant

gant houfes, gardens, vineyards, and corn fields: this country lies about thirty-five miles Eaft from the Cape Town.

6th, We afcended the mountains by an exceedingly fteep rugged path, which the peafants call Hottentot Holland Kloof [b], and after much labour and fatigue gained their fummit, when we entered a fpacious plain, interfperfed with an infinite number of large fragments of rocks, vifibly decayed by the force of the S.E. wind, which blows here during the fummer with very great force. Some of thefe rocks appeared like the ruins of church-fteeples, and were worn fo thin with wind and rain, that the fofter parts of them were perforated in many places. They are formed of the *cos quadrum* of LINNÆUS. The foil about them is a black earth intermixed with a pure white fand, probably proceeding from the decay of the rocks. Thefe mountains abound with a great number of curious plants, and are, I believe, the richeft mountains in Africa for a botanift. We then paffed the Palmet Rivier, fo called by the peafants from a plant [c] which almoft covers the water; the leaves of which greatly refemble that of the ananas or pineapple, but their flowers are like thofe of a reed. At night we croffed a fmall river, called Boter Rivier; and took up our lodging at a mean cottage, where the Dutchmen and Hottentots live almoft promifcuoufly together, their beds confifting only of fheep's fkins. The next morning an

(b) Kloof, is a narrow paffage over the lower part of a chain of mountains, or fometimes a narrow paffage between mountains.

(c) *Schoenus ferratus.*

old Hottentot brought out a fat wether, and flaughtered it; part of which we ate for our breakfaft.

8th, We came to a hot bath, fituated on the S.E. fide of a large mountain called Zwart Berg (d). The India Company have erected here a tolerable houfe for the reception of fick people. The water is fcalding hot where it fprings out of the earth; but after being conveyed about ten or twelve paces to the bath, it becomes more temperate. The people here feem to ufe it for all difeafes without exception, and often perhaps receive more hurt than benefit by it.

10th, We croffed Rivier Zonder Eynde; that is, Endlefs River, which difcharges itfelf into the Breed Rivier (e). At night we came to Sweet Milk Valley, where there is a good houfe belonging to the overfeer of the Company's woods; who received us with great civility, and kept us with him five days. The fourth day, we went into the woods, which are about half-way up a high chain of mountains that extends along the N. and N.E. fide of the the valley. I was accompanied by a farmer's fon, who took with him eight large rough dogs, which in our way ftarted two wolves; one of them we wounded with fmall fhot, fo that the dogs overtook him. A fierce battle enfued, which lafted an hour before he was killed. We afterwards climbed over many dreadful precipices till we arrived at the woods; which are dark and gloomy, interfperfed with climbing fhrubs of various kinds. The trees are very high; fome from eighty to a hundred feet;

(d) Black Mountain.	(e) Broad River.

often

often growing out of perpendicular rocks where no earth is to be feen. Among thefe the water fometimes falls in cafcades over rocks two hundred feet perpendicular, with awful noife. I endured this day much fatigue in thefe fequeftered and unfrequented woods, with a mixture of horror and admiration. The greateft part of the trees that compofe them are unknown to botanifts. Some I found in flower; others, which were not fo, I was obliged to leave for the refearches of thofe who may come after me in a more fortunate feafon.

16th, I vifited a Hottentot Kraal: the men were all, at this time, attending their herds; but the women and children were employed in building their huts; which are very low, of a circular figure, and made of flender poles, the ends of which are ftuck into the ground, fo as to form a number of arches croffing one another; thefe they afterwards cover with mats made of reeds. They have a round hole in the middle of the floor, in which they make the fire, and fit all round it upon the ground; but have no chimney or hole to let out the fmoke.

18th, We croffed the Breed Rivier, which is confider-able, and only paffable in winter by a ferry; but at this feafon we forded it at the place where the Rivier Zonder Eynde joins it. At night we arrived at Schwellendam, a place about 150 miles N.E. from the Cape Town, where we remained two days; but finding the feafon too far fpent for making any confiderable collections, I returned back to the Cape by the fame road I came. It was on this

journey

journey that I collected the feed of the many beautiful fpecies of *ericæ* which, I find, have fucceeded fo well in the Royal Garden at Kew.

---

# SECOND JOURNEY.

R. Feb. 22, 1776. **M**Y fecond journey was performed in company with Dr. THUNBERG, a native of Sweden; who was fent out by the Dutch to collect plants at the Cape, and is on that errand now in the Dutch Eaft Indies.

Sept. 11, 1773, We left the Cape Town, directing our courfe along the N.W. Coaft. We paffed the Blue Mountains; but the weather proving rainy, and attended with a fog, we loft our intended road, and were obliged to lodge that night in the fields.

12th, We came to Groene Kloof, a place belonging to the Eaft-India-Company, where we remained feveral days, the weather being rainy and unfettled; during which time we made feveral excurfions along the fides of the hills, and alfo over a large fandy defart towards the fea fhore; where we found a great variety of beautiful plants, and feveral animals peculiar to this climate; *viz.* antelopes, oftriches, and plovers of feveral forts.

19th, From Groene Kloof we paffed a fmall hill, called Konter Berg; and from thence entered a large barren country, named Zwart Land(*a*). The earth is a grey fand,

(*a*) Black Land.

level

level for many miles, and covered over with low fhrubs of various forts. At night we came to a farmer's houfe, where we remained two days, ranging the adjacent fields, in which we found many curious plants, and fhot feveral animals, as fteenbocken, hares, partridges.

22d, Still, in the fame direction, we travelled over a deep, fandy country with great fatigue; when, towards the evening, we arrived at Saldana Bay. Here we lodged with a farmer on the Eaft fide of the bay; but being defirous of croffing to a houfe inhabited by fome of the company's fervants, who during the fummer feafon fhoot feals for oil, on the 23d we made a fignal for them to fend their boat; which they immediately anfwered, and brought us over the bay, which is about two miles in breadth, where we were hofpitably entertained by the mafter. I obferved, that the direction of this bay is laid down wrong in all the maps that I have feen, except that of the Abbé DE LA CAILLE; they have given it a right Eaft direction, whereas it has nearly a South direction, almoft parallel to the feacoaft, and, I fuppofe, almoft twenty miles in length. The entrance of the bay is difficult, having feveral fmall iflands in it, and the adjacent country being little better than a fandy defart, and the water brackifh; it is, I think, improper for fhipping. It lies about fifty miles N.N.W. from the Cape Town. We found here great variety of curious plants; and in particular, a large bulbous root, growing on dry precipices, which the Dutch call *vergift-boll*, poifon bulb; the juice of which, they fay, the Hottentots ufe as an ingredient to poifon their arrows.

We

We found it to be a fpecies of *amaryllis*, and, by the leaves growing in a fan fhape, we called it *amaryllis difticha.*

27th, From Saldana Bay we journeyed to Witte Klip (White Cliff) being a white granite ftone of an enormous fize; from the top of which we had a charming view of the fea coaft from St. Helena Bay to the Cape of Good Hope. The whole country affords a fine field for botany, being enamelled with the greateft number of flowers I ever faw, of exquifite beauty and fragrance. Here we faw numbers of wild dogs, and fome of them fo near that I could difcern them to be about the fize of a large fox-hound. They go in large packs, and do great damage to the cattle. They alfo deftroy the antelopes wherever they go, by hunting them down in the fame manner as our hounds do a ftag.

30th, To St. Helena Bay, where the Berg Rivier difcharges itfelf, which is here very deep, and bordered on each fide by extenfive marfhes that are impaffable, and overgrown with very high reeds. Thofe reeds are plentifully ftocked with birds of various forts, which build their nefts upon fuch of them as hang over the water. There is one bird, in particular, which has a wonderful effect among the green reeds; its body being a bright crimfon, with black and grey wings; and by the brightnefs of their colours, when fitting among the reeds, they look like fo many fcarlet lillies: this is the *loxia orix* of LINNÆUS. There are ftill fome of the fea horfe, or *hippopotamus amphibius*, in this river; but it is now prohibited to fhoot

any

any of them, as they are nearly deſtroyed for 800 miles from the Cape. The farmers ſhoot them for their fleſh, which they eſteem as good as pork; and of their hide, which is extremely thick, they make whips. There happened at this time a great flood, that prevented our croſſing the river at this place, and obliged us to travel four days up the river to a ferry, which greatly retarded our journey, and occaſioned many difficulties by the deepneſs of the ſand and brackiſhneſs of the water; nor is there any wine or fruit in this part of the country, owing to the ſaltneſs of the ſoil.

Oct. 6th, We came to the pont or ferry, where we collected a great number of beautiful plants, particularly *ixiæ, irides,* and *gladioli.*

7th, We croſſed the Berg Rivier, and entered a fine plain country, called 24 Rivieren Diſtrict; ſo called from the number of ſmall rivulets which run through that diſtrict, and diſcharge into the Berg Rivier. Here we had ſome four wines, and oranges and lemons in great plenty.

9th, We paſſed a branch of that chain of mountains which I mentioned in my firſt journey. They continue for many miles further to the N.W. gradually diminiſhing in height to the Weſtern ſhore. This paſſage over the mountains is called Kartouw, and is remarked for being one of the moſt difficult in this part of Africa; which we found true, being obliged to lead our horſes for three hours amidſt inceſſant rain, which made the road ſo ſlippery that, by often tumbling among the looſe ſtones, they had their legs almoſt ſtripped of the ſkin;

ſkin; and the precipices were ſo ſteep, that we were often afraid to turn our eyes to either ſide. Towards ſun-ſet, with great labour and anxiety, we got ſafe to the other ſide, where we found a miſerable cottage belonging to a Dutchman. Being however cold and wet, we were glad to take refuge under his roof. The hut had only one room; but our hoſt gave us a corner to ſleep in, which was detached by a hanging of reed mats, where he and his wife alſo ſlept; and in the other end lay a number of Hottentots promiſcuouſly together.

10th, We croſſed the Olyfant's Rivier, nearly 130 miles North of the Cape Town, where we entered into a pleaſant valley, bounded on each ſide by very high mountains; thoſe on the Eaſt had their ſummits covered with ſnow, it being then their ſpring. This country produces good corn and European fruit in great plenty, eſpecially oranges and lemons in the greateſt profuſion; and the trees grow to a great ſize. They have alſo wine, but it is ſour and unwholeſome; which, I think, may be owing to their planting their vines in wet, marſhy places. The fruit yields watery juices, which ſeldom ripen, but produce good brandy. There is a hot bath here, which we viſited, iſſuing from the ſide of a mountain. The water was nearly boiling hot at the place it iſſued out of the rock; and the people who uſed it affirmed, that it was hot enough to boil a piece of meat. I obſerved an orange tree, which had been either raiſed from a ſingle ſeed, or planted when very young, in a ſeam of the rock where the water boiled out, which, to

5

my

my furprize flourifhed amazingly, and all the fides of the bafon where the people bathed were matted round with the fibres.

11th, 12th, 13th, 14th, We travelled along the banks of this river, making fhort ftages. The meadows yielded excellent pafture for our cattle, the grafs reaching up to their bellies, but of a coarfe texture, being chiefly *Juncus*, *fcirpus*, and *cyperus*.

15th, We attempted to crofs the high ridge of mountains on the North fide; but found it impracticable, having overturned our waggons on the fide of a precipice, and greatly damaged them, which obliged us to return to a peafant's houfe to get them repaired. This done, we held a confultation what courfe to take; and after fome warm debates, concluded to fend our waggons round to a place called Rood Land, there to wait for us, while the Doctor and I directed our courfe through a country called Koud Bocke Veld, or Cold Country of Antelopes; fo named from a fpecies of antelopes which inhabits here, called Spring bock. This animal when hunted, inftead of running, avails itfelf of furprizing fprings or leaps, which I fhall have occafion more particularly to mention hereafter.

17th, We directed our courfe Eaftward through Elans Kloof, a narrow winding paffage through a high chain of mountains, which lies to the N.E. of Olyfant's Rivier. This road is rugged beyond defcription, confifting of broken and fhattered rocks and rugged precipices, encompaffed on each fide with horrid impaffable mountains; the fides of which are covered with fragments of rocks that have tumbled down from the fummits at different times. We faw few plants here, only fome trees of the *protea grandiflora* thinly difperfed along the fkirts of thefe mountains. We croffed, in this paffage, feveral fmall rivers of the pureft water I ever beheld, which afforded us no fmall relief during the heat of the day. Towards the evening we entered the Koud Bocke Veld; and afterwards came to a peafant's houfe, where we remained that night.

18th, 19th, 20th, We travelled through the Koud Bocke Veld, where we found but few plants: the face of the country being exceedingly barren, and not fo much as a fhrub to be feen. The feafon here appeared to be two months later than in the neighbourhood of the Cape Town, although the diftance be not above a hundred miles, in a direct line in a Northern direction. This country is but fmall, containing about nine or ten Dutch places, the inhabitants of which fubfift intirely by their cattle. Their winters are often fo fevere, that the ground is covered with fnow for ten days together; and their early calves and lambs are often killed by the inclemency of the weather. Neither orange trees nor vines will live here, owing to the bleaknefs of its fituation; and the boors informed us, the fummers are often fo unkindly, that their wheat is blighted while in ear, fo that they purchafe corn with their cattle from the low country farmers. The country is encompaffed on all fides with very high mountains, almoft perpendicular, confifting of bare rocks, with-

out

out the leaſt appearance of vegetation; and upon the whole, has a moſt melancholy effect on the mind. We ſaw ſome herds of the ſpring-bocks, a ſpecies of antelope, as obſerved before, which were ſo ſhy, that we could not come within muſket-ſhot of them.

21ſt, We deſcended by a very ſteep path into another ſmall country, called Warm Bocke Veld, encompaſſed alſo on all ſides with horrid mountains, but not nearly ſo barren. Here we had ſome four wine and fruit; we were alſo delighted to ſee the luxuriance of the meadows, the graſs reaching to our horſes bellies, enriched with great variety of *ixiæ, gladioli* and *irides,* moſt of which were in flower at the Cape in the month of Auguſt.

22d, We had a high chain of mountains to paſs before we arrived at Rood Land, where we expected to meet our waggons. Upon inquiring about the road thither of the women, with whom we had lodged the preceding night, the men being all from home, ſo that we could not procure a guide; they informed us, there was only one paſs, called Moſtart's Hoek, which was very dangerous; and that, without a guide, we ſhould run the riſk of loſing our lives, having a rapid river ſeveral times to croſs, the fords of which, by the late rains, had been rendered more dangerous than uſual. We were a little intimidated by this information; but fortifying ourſelves with reſolution we proceeded, and in an hour arrived at the firſt precipice, where we looked down with horror on the river, which formed ſeveral cataracts inconceivably wild and

romantic,

romantic. This pafs, which took us near three hours march, is at the broadeft about a quarter of a mile, but in general not above an eighth part of one. The mountains on each fide rifing almoft perpendicular to a ftupendous height, had their fummits then covered with fnow, part of which remains till March. This river, which is the beginning of the Broad River, we had four times to crofs. The ford was exceedingly rough, the bed of the river being filled with huge ftones, which tumble down from the fides of the mountain; but we thought our labour and difficulties largely repaid by the number of rare plants we found here. The bank of the river is covered with great variety of evergreen trees; viz. *brabejum ftellatifolium, kiggelaria Africana, myrtus anguftifolia,* and the precipices are ornamented with *ericæ* and many other mountain plants never defcribed before. At night we arrived at Rood Land, where we found our fervants and waggons, and being a little fatigued we devoted the next day to reft and the examination of our plants. It is to be obferved, that during the preceding five days we had rather fhortened our diftance from the Cape, by reafon of the impoffibility of taking the waggons over the mountains with us; fo that we were now one day's journey nearer the Cape than we had been on Bocke Veld.

26th, We travelled up a high mountain, called Winter Hoek, on the N.W. of Rood Land, one of the higheft mountains in this part of Africa, whofe top is covered with fnow the greateft part of the year. Here we expected to find plants that might endure the feverity of

our

our climate; but when we arrived at its top, we found
nothing but a few graffes, *reſtiones, elegiæ*; the whole
mountain confifting of rock, lying in horizontal *ſtra-
ta*, without any fort of earth, except a little decayed
rock in which the graffes grew. From the foot of this
mountain to its fummit is a good day's journey, it
being very rugged and difficult to mount.. We found
many curious plants growing along the borders of the
ſtreams, which run in great plenty down the mountain's
ſide. Rood Land is a fine level country, furrounded
on all fides by lofty mountains, except on the Eaſt, where
the valley continues for feveral days journey inclofed
by mountains on each ſide. Thofe on the Northern fide
continue for feveral hundred miles in an oblique direction, and terminate on the Eaſtern coaſt. This country produces corn and wine in abundance, and moſt of
our European fruits, which have been planted there by
the new inhabitants, who are defcendants of the
French refugees; a civil, hofpitable, and induſtrious
people.

28th, 29th, We continued our journey along the
banks of the Broad River, where we collected many remarkably fine flowers, particularly one of the lilaceous
kind, with a long fpike of pendulous flowers, of a greeniſh
azure colour, which among the long grafs had an admirable effect (this is *ixia viridis*).

30th, We croffed the Hexen Rivier (Witches River),
which has a paffage through the mountains, and joins
the

the Broad River; this place is alſo remarkable for a hot bath.

31ſt, We paſſed on to Ko Aree Rivier, where we found many new plants; in particular, *gerania* and *ſtapeliæ.*

Nov. 2d, To Koekman's Rivier, the banks of which are covered with thick woods, and furniſhed with a variety of birds, which afforded us good ſport. The trees were moſtly of the *mimoſa nilotica* of LINNÆUS; the ſpecies of the birds I have not yet determined, not being provided with books upon Ornithology to ſettle one half of thoſe which I collected on this journey.

5th, We arrived at Swellendam, deſcribed in my firſt journey; and the ſame day dined with the Land Droſt, who is a juſtice of peace, and collects different taxes from the peaſants. After dinner we purſued our route to Buffel Tagt's Rivier, where is a place belonging to the Eaſt India Company. There they keep a few wood-cutters, and from thence ſupply the wheelers at the Cape, conveying their wood in waggons drawn by oxen: this place, I think, is about 150 miles from the Cape. Here we reſted five days for the benefit of our oxen, which had become very lean, and the Doctor got a freſh ſet out of the Eaſt India Company's herd.

10th, To Davenhoek's Rivier, where we remained all night, and the next morning proceeded on our journey. The Doctor imprudently took the ford without the leaſt inquiry; when on a ſudden, he and his horſe plunged over head and ears into a pit, that had been made by the *hippopotamus amphibius,* which formerly inhabited

habited thofe rivers. The pit was very deep, and fteep on all fides, which made my companion's fate uncertain for a few minutes; but, after feveral ftrong exertions, the horfe gained the oppofite fide with his rider.

12th, To Caffer Kuyl's Rivier. Upon our left hand, a few miles diftant, we had the chain of mountains before mentioned, which here take a N.E. direction. Their fummits terminate in a number of lofty, rugged pieces, which have an admirable effect. Between this chain of mountains and the fea on the S.E. lies an extenfive country, to appearance low; but when one travels acrofs it, it prefents a continued feries of hills and dales. The hills are quite fmooth and eafy of afcent, and covered with long coarfe grafs, which cattle feldom eat. On the declivities of thefe low hills grows the *aloe Socotorina* in large clumps, which when old have ftems about five or fix feet high, with only a few thick leaves on their tops, that at a diftance appear like bands of Hottentots. The peafants make great quantities of the gum aloes from the fap of the leaves, which they fell at the Cape from two to fix pence *per* pound. There is a fine fpecies of antelope, which inhabits only here, called by the peafants Bonte Bock; fomething larger than a fallow deer, very fhy, but not very fwift.

15th, To Goud's Rivier; which at that time was about 100 yards broad, and the water came up to the feat of our faddles. On each fide of this river lies an extraordinary track of land, which in the Hottentot language is called Carro. It is a dry, burning foil, of a reddifh colour,

intermixed

intermixed with rotten rock, and intirely divefted of grafs; but enriched with an infinite number of evergreen fhrubs, both frutefcent and fucculent: among the latter we found many new fpecies of *craffula, cotyledon, euphorbia, portulaca, mefembryantbemum.* We refolved to vifit the fea fhore, and particularly Moffel-Baay; when, late in the evening, we came to the houfe of an European, who received us very hofpitably. He was a native of Swedifh Pomerania, about feventy years old; had been fhipwrecked on the coaft of England fifty years ago, and fpoke much of the hofpitality of the Englifh. He was a man of learning, and expreffed many fenfible reflexions on the tyranny of his native country, which had forced him to feek for an afylum in the defarts of Africa. His houfe was very mean, built of mud, and miferably furnifhed; not having a bed to lie on, though he had feveral hundred oxen and fome thoufands of fheep. He had a number of Hottentot vaffals, whofe huts were fituated round his folds, where they kept feveral large fires all night long, to frighten away the wolves and tigers.

16th, We came to Moffel-Baay, which is very large, open, and expofed to the S.E. and E. The fhore is covered with fhrubs of various kinds; the greateft part of which were unknown to us, and many we did not find in flower. To the N.E. of Moffel-Baay lies a woody country, called Houtniquas Land; whofe woods, intercepted by rivers and precipices, are fo large, that their extent is not perfectly known. Thefe woods are a great treafure to the Dutch, and will be very ferviceable to the

S                                                inhabitants

inhabitants of the Cape, when their other woods are ex-hauſted. In them are numbers of wild buffaloes that are very fierce, and ſome elephants; which renders travelling dangerous. We now directed our courſe Northward to the foot of the great chain of mountains, which we had again to croſs; it is there very broad, being a hard day's march from one ſide to the other. This paſs is called by the peaſants Hartiquas Kloof.

19th, We were ſeveral hours in aſcending, and after deſcending on the other ſide, we entered a valley, ſur-rounded by lofty mountains: here we reſted that night by a ſtream of water, where we collected many curious plants.

20th, We continued our journey through a diſmal valley, where we ſaw neither man nor beaſt; but our la-bour was generouſly rewarded by the productions of the vegetable kingdom, having found ſeveral new ſpecies of plants, which for neatneſs and elegance exceeded any thing I had ever ſeen. At night we got clear of the mountains, but entered a rugged country, which the new inhabitants name Canaan's Land; though it might rather be called the Land of Sorrow; for no land could exhibit a more waſteful proſpect; the plains conſiſting of nothing but rotten rock, intermixed with a little red loam in the interſtices, which ſupported a variety of ſcrubby buſhes, in their nature evergreen, but, by the ſcorching heat of the Sun, ſtripped almoſt of all their leaves. Yet notwithſtanding the diſagreeable aſpect of this tract, we enriched our collection by a variety of succulent plants, which we had never seen before, and which appeared to us like a new creation.

21st, To Great Thorn River, where we encamped under a large *mimosa* tree. During the night, we had several loud claps of thunder with rain.

22d, We entered Lange Kloof, which is a narrow valley, not exceeding two miles at the broadest, and in length about 100; bounded on the S.W. by the chain of mountains beforementioned, and on the North and East by a lower ridge, which runs nearly parallel. It contains about seven or eight places, which are from twelve to twenty miles distant from each other; the houses are very mean, without walls, consisting only of poles stuck in the ground, meeting at the top, and thatched over with reeds. The people, however, are wealthy, possessing large herds and flocks. The Hottentots are in general servants to the Dutch farmers; who give them for wages beads, and tobacco mixed with hemp; the latter, which intoxicates them, they are extremely fond of. A few free Hottentots still remain here, who live in their ancient manner; but who are miserable wretches, having hardly any stock of cattle.

29th, To Kromme Rivier (that is, Crooked River) a long, marshy vale, which lies much lower than the former, and is bounded by a continuation of the abovementioned mountains.

30th,

30th, To Effe Bofch, where we encamped that night in the open fields, clear of the woods, for fear of the lions.

Dec. 1ft, We entered a fine level country, bordering on the Eaftern Ocean, leaving behind us the chain of mountains before mentioned, which runs obliquely acrofs the country from the Atlantic to the Indian Ocean. At night we came to Zee-Koe Rivier, or Sea-Cow River, fo called, erroneoufly, from the *hippopotamus amphibius*, which formerly inhabited it, but is now almoft extirpated. We refted here eight days; in which time we ranged the adjacent woods and fields, where we greatly increafed our collection. The river was frequented by a variety of water-fowl which afforded us good fport: there were numbers of the *phenocopterus ruber, pelicanus onocrotalus*, with many others, which we could not clafs, being un- provided, as I faid, with books of Ornithology. We lodged at the houfe of JACOB KOCK, an old German, who ufed us with great civility. He had built a handfome houfe, made gardens and vineyards, poffeffed numerous herds of cattle, and had upwards of a hundred Hottentots in his fervice, whom he employed in taking care of them. The face of the country changes greatly, being open, plain, and covered with verdure, extending many miles along the fea-coaft, containing feveral tribes of Hottentots. The rivers formerly abounded with the *hip- popotamus amphibius*; but fince the Dutch inhabited thefe parts, they have almoft deftroyed them. They fhoot

them

them for their flefh, which they efteem equal to pork,
their fat being much of the fame quality.  The
manner in which the Hottentots catch thefe animals
is as follows: the banks of the rivers, as I have already
obferved, are covered with almoft impenetrable woods;
thefe animals in the day time lodge themfelves in the
deepeft places of the river, and when night comes,
make excurfions into the adjacent fields to graze, taking
their courfe through paths, which they have made in
the woods.  In thefe paths the Hottentots dig large pits,
which they cover over with boughs of trees and grafs;
then hunting them out of the fields, the animals make
full-fpeed towards the river, and fall into thefe pits; from
whence they are unable to get out, on account of their
great weight, and then the men come up with their
lances and kill them.  We found here a new palm, of the
pith of which the Dutchman told us the Hottentots make
bread; but we could get no fatisfactory account of their
method of making it.  We obferved two fpecies; one
about a foot and a half diameter in the ftem, and about
twelve feet high, with entire leaves; they appeared to be
very old, and feldom bore fruit.  The other fort had no
ftem, with the leaves a little ferrated, and lying flat on
the ground, which produced a large conical fructification
about eighteen inches long, and a foot or more in cir-
cumference; fquamofe, and under each of the *fquamæ*, is
an oval nut, about the fize of a chefnut, of a beautiful
red colour, but infipid tafte.  The male plant is fimilar

to

to the female, only not producing fruit, but bearing a *ftrobulus*, and containing the *pollen*, or male-duft, in fmall cells underneath its *fquamæ.* In the woods here we found the *euphorbia antiquorum* forty feet high. The inhabitants obferve, that the honey found near thefe trees is unwholefome. Being ftill determined to continue our journey about 150 miles further, directing our courfe towards the middle of the country, and to return to the Cape another way; I furnifhed myfelf with a fet of frefh oxen and a fortnight's provifion; and Mr. ROCK gave us one of his fons for a guide and to ferve us as interpreter, he being a perfect mafter of the Hottentot language.

9th, We took leave of our hofpitable friend, and departing towards the evening, we ftopped that night at the houfe of JACOB VAN RENNEN, a wealthy grazier: this was the laft Dutch place in this part of the country. From hence we travelled through a rugged hilly country, covered with thick coppices of evergreen trees; but the way was fo rough that our waggons were almoft fhaken to pieces. Towards noon we croffed Camtour's River, where we refted during the heat of the day, and amufed ourfelves in the woods along its banks, which were extremely pleafant: the river is broad and deep in many places. The woods are frequented by elephants, buffaloes, and lions; and the deepeft parts of the river by the *hippopotami.* We found many new plants here, notwithftanding our ftay was fo fhort. In the afternoon we advanced

through

through a woody country, where we obferved numbers of butterflies, which appeared like thofe of India; but from the thicknefs of the woods we could not procure a fingle fpecimen. At night we came to Lory's River, fo called from a fpecies of parrot, which is found here. We were vifited by feveral Hottentots, who came out of the woods armed with lances, but behaved very obligingly, and flept by our fire all night; and we at the fame time entertained them with tobacco, of which they were exceedingly fond.

11th, We travelled over a pleafant country, diverfified with fmooth green hills, interfperfed with evergreens, and ftocked with numerous flocks of the *capra dorcas* of LINNÆUS, *equus zebra,* and *camelus ftruthio*; which, together with the fine difpofition of the woods and groves, could not but charm us, who, for upwards of three months, had been climbing rugged mountains, and croffing fultry defarts. In the evening we came to Van Staad's Rivier, where we remained all night, and were vifited by feveral Hottentots, who brought us milk in bafkets made of fine reeds, which they weave fo clofe that they hold any liquid.

12th, We croffed Van Staad's Rivier, where there is a large Kraal, or Hottentot village, containing upwards of 200 inhabitants, who are poffeffed of great herds of bullocks, but of no fheep. Thefe Hottentots were remarkably well-fhaped, and ftouter made than any other Hottentots I have yet feen. They are alfo very bold in

3                                                    encountering

encountering wild beasts, particularly the lion, which often attacks their folds, and makes great havock. When this happens, all the young men of the Kraal go in purfuit of him, directed by fmall dogs, who follow his fcent: as foon as they difcover him in the bufhes, they irritate him, till he fprings out with fury and attacks them; when being all armed with haffagays, they often throw twenty or thirty into his body at once; but it is common to lofe a man or two in fuch attacks. Thefe Hottentots were all cloathed in *croffes*, or mantles, made of the hides of oxen, which they drefs in a particular manner, making them as pliant as a piece of cloth: they wore the hairy fide outwards. Their breaft, belly, and thighs, were naked, except being croffed by a number of leathern ftraps round their middle. They had no other covering for their private parts, than a muzzle of leather exactly covering the extremity of the *penis*, and fufpended by a leathern thong from their girdle, which was commonly ornamented with brafs rings. Some had the fkin of a fteenbock hung over their breaft, with the fkin of its fore legs and hoofs behind, which they look upon as a great ornament; others had a buffalo's tail, faftened to a girdle which was tied round the thigh; others a porcupine's quill ftuck through each ear; others had plates of brafs of fix inches fquare faftened to their hair, hanging on each fide of their head; others large ivory rings round their arms, with feveral other ridiculous fancies too tedious to mention. The women were dreffed almoft in the fame tafte, except that a great number of fmall thongs of leather, fufpended

from

from their girdle, reached down to their knees, and in fome meafure concealed their nakednefs.    They have captains or chiefs over each Kraal, who claim the greateft part of the herds; the others feem only to be fervants, though they have every thing in common, and pay little refpect to their fuperiors.    Thefe Hottentots are called Gunaquas, but were mixed with another people whom the Dutch call Caffers, who border upon Terra de Natal.    They were all armed with haffaguays, of which every one had eight or ten in his left hand.    We found here the true Cape jaffemine, or *gardenia ftellata*, and the coral tree, *erethrina corallodendron*.    The climate here differs much from that of the Cape.    They have no S.E. wind, which is fo troublefome there; their ftrongeft wind is from the S.W.    They feldom have rain in fummer, though often thunder and lightning; the clouds being attracted by the lofty mountains are fpent in fhowers before they reach the plain.

13th, 14th, We made but very fhort ftages, employing our time in collecting plants, all of which were new.    The buffalo is numerous in this country: it is a fierce animal, and larger than the biggeft of our Englifh oxen.    In the day-time they retire to the woods, which renders it very dangerous to botanize there.    We here faw two lions for the firft time, at about 4 or 500 yards diftance; but they took no notice of us, keeping their eyes upon a clump of the *capra dorcas*, which were feeding at fome diftance from them.    We fhot two of the buffaloes which proved good eating.

7

15th, To Zwart Kop's Rivier, where we refted all night.

16th, To Zwart Kop's Salt-pan, where we remained moft part of that day. This Salt-pan is a lake feveral miles diftant from the fea, and upon an eminence. In the rainy feafon it is filled with frefh water, which, by the faltnefs of the ground, foon becomes ftrongly impregnated with faline particles; and when the fummer's heat exhales the frefh water, the bottom of the lake is covered with a cruft of pure falt two or three feet thick. The lake is about three miles round, and furrounded by a rifing ground, covered with a great variety of curious fhrubs, many of which proved new. Here we found feveral fingular infects, and among many others the *gryllus* and *cimex*.

17th, We travelled through a miferable parched country, covered with fhrubs and fucculent plants of various kinds; but the grafs was entirely burnt up by the heat of the Sun. We faw numbers of wild animals, and in particular a variety of the Zebra, called by the Hottentots Opeagha. We alfo obferved the print and dung of elephants and lions. At noon we came to Sunday's River, where we refted a few hours, and confulted with our guide, whom we took from the laft Dutch place, about proceeding on our journey. But both he and our fervants refufed to advance further; telling us, we were now on the borders of a powerful nation of Hottentots, called Caffers; who, they faid, would kill us, were it only to get the iron belonging to our waggons. In confequence of thefe remonftrances, and the bad ftate our carriages were in, being ready to drop to pieces, and many of our oxen fick, we, with much reluctance, confented to return the fame way we came.

20th, We arrived again at Sea-cow River, where we rapaired our waggons.

24th, 28th, We proceeded homewards through Kromme Rivier and part of Lange Kloof; but being informed there was a hot bath about a day's journey to the Northward, we determined to fee it, leaving our waggons and fervants in Lange Kloof.

29th, Towards the evening we croffed the ridge of mountains on the North-fide of Lange Kloof, and at night came to a folitary cottage belonging to a Dutchman, where we found feveral Dutch people, who were going next day to the hot bath, to ufe the water. We were glad of their company, and travelled over the drieft country I ever beheld. The plains were covered with loofe ftones, and not a blade of grafs to be feen; but we found many rare fpecies of *craffula*, *mefembryanthemum*, and other fucculent plants. In fome places not a drop of water was to be found within thirty miles circuit. We could of courfe expect to fee but few animals; thofe were the *capra dorcas*, *equus zebra*, *kocdoes*, and fpringbocks.

30th, At night we arrived at the hot bath, which is fituated at the foot of a ridge of dry mountains: the water is very hot, and taftes ftrongly of iron. There is a Dutch fettlement about 300 yards from the fountain, where they float their gardens every night with

the

the water, which at that diſtance is ſtill ſmoaking. By this means they have all kind of garden vegetables in the greateſt perfection. Next morning we went up to the top of this ridge of mountains, which appeared like a maſs of rocks heaped one on top of another, where we had an extenſive view of the country, which appeared horrible, every thing being parched up, and even the beds of the largeſt rivers entirely dry. We found here a ſpecies of heath remarkable for having its branches and leaves all covered with a fine hoary down or nap, which we thought ſingular in that *genus:* we called it *erica tomentoſa.*

Jan. 1ſt, We returned to Lange Kloof, and next day overtook our waggons; but many of our oxen were ſick, having caught a diſeaſe which rages there amongſt the horned cattle in ſummer, and ſo affects their hoofs that they often drop off, and great numbers die. This diſeaſe proves detrimental to the Dutch peaſants, who live 5 or 600 miles in the country, when they make a journey to the Cape. Their oxen are often ſeized with it in the middle of a deſart, and ſometimes muſt remain there for a month till they recover. This makes their journies to the Cape long and diſagreeable, eſpecially as they are obliged to take with them their wives and children, for fear of their being murdered by the Hottentots in their abſence.

3d, We came to Great Thorney River, where we again parted with our waggons, in order to examine a large tract of Carro, where it was improper to take our oxen on account of the fcarcity of water. Late in the after-noon we came to a peafant's houfe, who informed us, he had a neighbour about four hours ride from his place, by whom we fhould be kindly received, and who would further direct us on our journey. After having put us in the road, and given us fome directions, he parted with us, and we purfued our journey till fun-fet, but found no habitation. We therefore concluded, that we had cer-tainly loft our way, and returned fome miles back, where we found a road which branched off another way. In this path we continued till one o'clock in the morning, having got into a difmal valley, inclofed on each fide with rugged precipices: at laft we found ourfelves in the middle of a thicket of thorn trees *(mimofa nilotica)* where we unfaddled our horfes and kindled a fire. We paffed the night with little comfort, having eaten nothing all that day; but to our great fatisfaction we heard the murmuring of a ftream, which we went in fearch of, and found good water: our concern, however, was ftill great for our poor horfes that had nothing to eat. We fpent the night in gathering wood and keeping our fire up till day-light, when I climbed up a high precipice, and viewed the country. Here I collected feveral curious plants, *geranium fpinofum, ftapelia euphorbioides;* and upon my return, we mounted our horfes, and directed our courfe towards the high mountains, where we ex-pected to find fome relief, but were difappointed; for after being parched up with infupportable heat, we met not with a drop of water to quench our thirft

2

during

during the whole day's journey. But towards the evening we happily difcovered a houfe, where we were kindly entertained, and the next morning overtook our waggons in Hartwig's Kloof; but our oxen were in a bad ftate, and one of them was quite unfit for fervice We continued our journey without any other remarkable event, except that of lofing more of our oxen by the above mentioned difeafe.

12th, Came to Buffels Tagt River, where we refted feveral days, ranging the adjacent woods, where we found many curious trees in bloom.

29th, We arrived at the Cape Town, after a journey of four months and fourteen days.

---

## THIRD JOURNEY.

R. Feb. 29, 1776. SEPT. 26, 1774, I fet out from the Cape Town, but by the badnefs of the weather was obliged to ftay all night at the Salt River, about two miles from the town, where there is a wine-houfe. I had in company only two fervants, for driving my waggon and taking care of my oxen and horfe.

27th, The morning being fine we travelled through the great fandy plain (lying between the Cape Town and Hottentots Holland Mountains) great part of which was under water. In the afternoon we had heavy rain, when

we

we croſſed the Eerſte Rivier, and lodged all night at a farm-houſe under thoſe mountains, were we found the whole country enamelled with flowers.

28th, 30th, The weather began to grow more pleaſant, the Sun ſhining out with force; but ſudden heavy ſhowers much retarded our journey, confining us to ſhort ſtages along the foot of the Stelleboſch Mountains.

Oct. 1ſt, To Draaken Steen.

2d, To Paarle Kerk, where I was joined by Dr. THUNBERG.

4th, We went up to the top of the Paarle Mountain, where we added greatly to our collection.

5th, To Paarde Berg (Horſe Mountain).

6th, We mounted to the top of Paarde Berg, where we found a treaſure of new plants, which we had not ſeen before, and on the top had an extenſive view of the adjacent country, which is level, and has but a barren appearance; yet contains ſeveral rich plantations, producing abundance of corn and wine; and the peaſants live luxuriouſly. Their plantations lie all around the foot of this mountain, which yields a number of fine rivulets, without which this country would be uninhabited.

7th, We directed our courſe Northward, through a level country covered with low ſhrubs; but it being now ſpring, it was every where decorated with flowers of the greateſt beauty, every hour's march producing new charms. At night we arrived at the foot of a mountain called Van Riebeck's Caſteel. There we lodged at Mr. DRAYER's, a
wealthy

wealthy farmer, who treated us in the moſt friendly manner, and begged that we would favour him with our company for a month, which ſhould not coſt us a far-thing.

9th, We went up to the top of Riebeck's Caſteel, which is very high, and on the North ſide inacceſſible. It is about four or five miles long, and very narrow on the top; we collected here many remarkable new plants, in particular a hyacinth, with flowers of a pale gold eo-lour.

10th, We came to the Berg Rivier, which was then impaſſable by reaſon of the late rain.

12th, With ſome difficulty we tranſported, in a large boat, our waggons and baggage to the oppoſite ſide, and afterwards obliged our oxen to ſwim over. From thence we proceeded through a barren uninhabited country; conſequently were obliged to content ourſelves with the ſhelter of a large *leucodendron*, that protected us from the S.E. wind, which at this ſeaſon ſometimes blows cold.

13th, We arrived at the foot of a mountain called Piquet Berg, lying direct North from the Cape Town, being a particular place of obſervation of the Abbe DE LA CAILLE, when he meaſured a degree on the meridian in the year 1750. All around the mountain the ſoil is ſandy, but furniſhed with a great variety of beautiful plants, eſpecially *aſpalathi*.

15th, We mounted the Piquet Berg, which is very high but eaſy of aſcent. On the top are fine plains co-

vered

vered with excellent verdure, which are of great fervice to the peafants, who fend up their oxen during the fummer feafon. We faw here feveral zebras and two colts, but they were very fhy.

18th, We came to Verloore Valley, which begins on the N.W. fide of the Piquet Berg. It is a narrow extent of marfhy ground, inclofed by hills on each fide, with a fmall river, frequented by a variety of water fowl, which afforded good fport. Towards the fea, the river increafes in breadth, in many places upwards of a mile, and is very deep; there we faw hundreds of pelicans and wild geefe, which kept the middle of the river; but we fhot feveral wild ducks and water hens, which fwam among the reeds along the fide of it.

23d, We arrived at the mouth of the Verloore River, where it is difcharged into the fea; but found the coaft barren, confifting of fandy hills, fo loofe that our horfes were fometimes up to their bellies, which made our journey very fatiguing.

23d, We left the fhore on our left hand, and directed our courfe Northward towards the mouth of the Olyfant's Rivier. The heat became now great, which the whitenefs of the fand ftill increafed, and obliged us to travel late in the evening and early in the morning, refting in the middle of the day. It was alfo not a little fatiguing to travel here on horfeback, the mole-cafts being fo deep that the horfes fell up to their fhoulders every fix or feven minutes. This animal is by the Dutch called Landmoll, but differs fo much from the European mole, that

it

It does not belong to the fame clafs of animals, but is intirely new. It feeds upon the roots of *ixiæ, gladioli, antholyzæ,* and *irides,* often grows to the fize of a rabbit, and by fome is efteemed good eating. There is another fpecies of the animal, called by the Dutch Bles-moll, which inhabits the hard ground; but feldom exceeds the fize of the common European mole. This country is furnifhed with a great variety of elegant fhrubs; viz. *enifta, partia,* and *afpalathi.* At night we came to Lange Valley, where we took up our lodging in a defolate place, the inhabitants being all removed; for this is only their winter refidence, when the water is frefh, which had now began to be brackifh.

24th, We fet out early in the morning, expecting to find a river or fountain, where we could reft during the heat of the day; but, to our no fmall difappointment, we travelled till noon without finding any: our oxen were fo hot that their tongues hung out of their mouths. About one o'clock we faw a lake of water at fome diftance, but on our arrival our horfes refufed to drink: we difmounted, and found it to be a falt lake. In the evening we came to a fountain of excellent water, where we fpent the night with great comfort. Next morning we were vifited by a peafant going to the Cape; who told us, he had been attacked in the night by a lion, which made a fpring at his Hottentot who led the oxen, but happily miffed him. He admonifhed us to be expeditious, and get to fome habitation that night, otherwife we might expect a vifit from him.

25th, At noon we proceeded on our journey, the road continuing ftill very bad; and in paffing along we faw the prints of the lion's feet in feveral places. At night we came to Olyfant's Rivier, where we found a Dutch habitation; there we refted feveral days, being treated with great hofpitality. This country abounds with game. They have two kinds of partridges, which are exceedingly plentiful and eafy to fhoot; and a perfon cannot walk ten paces without raifing a brace of quails. Their hares are of an extraordinary fize, but differ little otherwife in character from thofe of Europe. We hunted every day, and by the affiftance of the peafant's fon, who was an excellent markfman, never failed to come home loaden. The fteril appearance of this country exceeds all imagination: wherever one cafts his eyes, he fees nothing but naked hills, without a blade of grafs, only fmall fucculent planrs. The foil is a red binding loam, intermixed with a kind of rotten *fchiftus* or flate. Next morning we traverfed the adjacent hills, and were furprized to find all the plants entirely new to us. They were the greateft part of the fucculent kind; viz. *mefembryanthemum, euphorbia,* and *ftapelia,* of which we found many new fpecies. The peafant told us, that in winter the hills were painted with all kind of colours; and faid, it grieved him often, that no perfon of knowledge in botany had ever had an opportunity of feeing his country in the flowery feafon. We expreffed great furprize at feeing fuch large flocks of fheep as he was poffeffed of fubfift in fuch a defart; on which he obferved,

that

that their sheep never ate any grass, only succulent plants, and all sorts of shrubs; many of which were aromatic, and gave their flesh an excellent flavour. Next day I passed through a large flock of sheep, where I saw them devouring the juicy leaves of *mesembryanthemum, stapelia, cotyledon*, and even the green seed vessels of *euphorbia*; by eating such plants they require little water, especially in winter.

30th, We were employed in unloading our waggons, and transporting our baggage across the river in a small boat; and afterwards drove over our oxen with the empty waggons, which were almost overset in the middle of it. The river is about forty or fifty yards broad, and in some places very deep. The borders are covered with the *mimosa nilotica*, which forms a thick impenetrable wood. We were about a day's journey from the mouth of this river, where are still some elephants remaining, the country being very wild and uninhabited. We had now the great Carro to pass; a desart of three days journey, where no fresh water, and only three pits of brackish water, enough to preserve the lives of our cattle, were to be found. These pits are at some distance from the road, which makes it very difficult for strangers to find them. But while we were seriously considering these approaching difficulties, thinking, if we should miss the pits, we should probably perish in this inhospitable desart, to our great joy we were overtaken by a Boor, with his wife and children, who were going the same road; but he having a fresh team of horses, we could not keep up with him.

However,

However, he directed us in the way; and told us, he would
tye a piece of white cloth on a branch of a tree, where
he knew there was water; but defired us not to go to
thofe places without fire-arms, as there was commonly a
lion lurking near them; who knowing that all the animals
muft come there to drink, he feldom failed to feize his
prey. At night we overtook our fellow traveller, who
had taken up his lodging on a bare eminence, without a
bufh to fhelter him; though at fome diftance there was a
fmall wood of *mimofa* trees along the banks of a river
that was then dry, which we thought much preferable
to his fituation. But he told us, it was much more dangerous on account of wild beafts; and that there often
fell fuch fudden fhowers in the mountains, that people who had lodged by the rivers, had, with their waggons and oxen, been carried away in the night while
they lay afleep. He left us early next morning, but we
were obliged to ftay till noon to let our oxen feed, and
then went on until fun-fet; but unhappily found no
water, which mortified us much, having a long day's
journey to the next watering place.      All next day
we travelled over this thirfty land, where we fuffered
from the heat of the Sun and want of water; but our
fufferings were ftill aggravated when we thought on
our poor animals, who often lay down in the yoke
during the heat of the day. This defart is extenfive;
being bounded on the N. and N.E. by a chain of flat
mountains, called Bockland's Bergen (Bockland's Mountains) and on the W. and N.W. by the Atlantic Ocean.

                                                   It

It is uninhabitable in fummer; but in winter, or during the rainy feafon, the Bockland people come down with their herds, which by feeding upon fucculent fhrubs, that are very falt, in a fhort time grow remarkably fat. There ftill remains a great treafure of new plants in this country, efpecially of the fucculent kind, which cannot be preferved but by having good figures and defcriptions of them made on the fpot; which might be eafily accomplifhed in the rainy feafon, when there is plenty of frefh water every where. But at this feafon of the year, we were obliged to make the greateft expedition to fave the lives of our cattle, only collecting what we found growing along the road fide, which amounted to above 100 plants, never before defcribed. Towards the evening we arrived at the foot of Bockland's Berg, where we paffed the night by a penurious ftream of frefh water, but which yielded us no fmall comfort.

Nov. 2d, The peafant who had paffed us in the Carro, as foon as he arrived at home, immediately fent two team of frefh oxen to help us up the mountain, our own being much weakened by the heavy roads. In the cool of the afternoon we afcended by a winding road, which was fo very rugged and fteep, that it took five hottentots with ropes made faft to the waggon to keep it from overturning. The face of the mountain confifts intirely of fcattered rock, being acceffible only in this place, and is overgrown with a great variety of large woody plants, moft of which were new. We found a new fpecies of aloe here, called by the Dutch Koker

5
Boom,

Boom, of which the Hottentots make quivers to hold their arrows; it being of a foft fibrous confiftence, which they can eafily cut out, leaving only the bark, which is hard and durable. Thefe trees were about twelve feet high, with a ftrait fmooth trunk, about ten inches or a foot diameter and five or fix feet in length, which divided into two branches; and thofe were again fub-divided into two more branches, which terminated in a bunch of thick fucculent leaves furrounding the ftem, fpear-fhaped, entire, without fpines, and hanging down like the leaves of *dracæna draco.* We did not fee it in flower, but by the above charaćters took it for a new fpecies, and called it *aloe dichotoma.* We gained the top of the mountain, and entered into Bockland, which is extended along the fummit for many miles. It is pretty level, but very rocky. We enjoyed a pure cool air, it being feveral degrees colder here than in the Carro. Bockland lies nearly in a Northern direćtion from the Cape, and at the diftance of about 220 miles. It was called Bockland on account of the amazing quantity of fpring bucks which were formerly found there; but fince this country has been inhabited by Europeans, it has ceafed to be the fettled refidence; at leaft, the number of thofe which conftantly remain in it is very inconfiderable. It generally happens, however, once in feven or eight years, that flocks of many hundred thoufands come out of the interior parts of Africa, fpreading over the whole country, and not leaving a blade of grafs or a fhrub. The peafants are then obliged to guard their corn fields night and day, otherwife thofe animals would caufe a famine wherever they paffed.

paffed. It feems probable, by the accounts of thefe extraordinary emigrations, that their natural habitation is in the interior parts of Terra de Natal; and that they are forced Southwards by dry feafons, which happen fometimes in thofe regions to fuch a degree, that not a drop of rain will fall for two or three years together. Thefe great flocks are faid to be always attended by lions; and it is obferved, where a lion is, there is a large open fpace. We faw feveral flocks, but not exceeding twenty in each. We met a party of Dutchmen, who had been about 150 miles to the Northward of Bockland, deftroying the Bofchman Hottentots. They informed us, they had feen great flocks of the fpring bucks; but there happening much rain, which had recovered the grafs and vegetation, they had been obferved to change their courfe, and return to the interior parts of the country.

3d, 4th, We continued our journey along this elevated tract; having on our right hand, or South-fide, the precipice, which is inacceffible; and on the North-fide, a defolate hilly country, inhabited by a few wandering tribes of the Bofchman Hottentots. At night we came to the place of our benefactor, whofe name was KLAAS LOSPER; he was a very opulent man in thofe parts, having upwards of 12000 fheep and 3000 bullocks. Moft of the plants that we collected here were new; and, I believe, many more remain, this having been the dry feafon, when moft of the flowers were gone.

6th, We directed our courfe Northward, through a dry, barren country, called Hantum; and on the 10th

came

came to the laft Dutch habitation on this fide of the country. As we paffed along we found many new plants growing near the banks of rivers, which were then quite dry; but the foil confifted of nothing but rotten rock. The hills were of the fame fubftance, all of a conical figure, and entirely covered with pieces of rock, about the fize of a man's fift. We continued feveral days at this habitation, where we were well entertained. They had excellent bread, good mutton, butter and milk, but no kind of ftrong liquors. We made feveral enquiries about the country lying to the Northward; and were told, that it had been formerly inhabited by Europeans near a hundred miles further, who at firft had greatly increafed their herds; but that fome dry feafons coming on afterwards, they had been forced to return: the country therefore was fuppofed to be uninhabited, except by the wandering Hottentots, who feldom ftay above a month in a place. This place is about 350 Englifh miles North from the Cape of Good Hope. We now changed our courfe, going directly S.E. through an uninhabited country much like the former, furrounded by high mountains, flat on the tops, and forming what the peafants call Table Mountains. I never faw the fmalleft rivulet or fountain iffuing from them; all the water that we found being that which was left ftagnant in the deepeft parts of the rivers, that are formed by the rain in the winter feafon, which rivers, towards Midfummer, in other places become entirely dry.

14th, To Rhinoceros Rivier. Here we faw great herds of zebras, and were informed by three Dutchmen, who paffed us on horfeback, that this place was frequented

quented by a large lion; and, as a proof, they shewed us a zebra, which he had lately killed; assuring us, if we stayed all night there, he would pay us a visit. We travelled about ten miles further, and at night saw a flock of sheep and some bullocks, which greatly animated us, expecting to find some habitation where we might shelter ourselves during the night; but, when we came to the place where the sheep were, we found a Dutchman with his wife and several young children sitting under the shelter of some bushes, which they had formed into an alcove, to skreen them from the heat of the Sun. We stayed here all night, and the man asked us to sup with them; which we did, and made them a present of some tea and tobacco, which they thankfully received; and the next day the husband saddled his horse, rode six or seven miles with us, and gave us very good directions how to proceed in our intended course.

16th, We ascended a flat chain of mountains, called Rogge Velds Berg, where we found the road extremely rugged. Rogge Veld extends along the summit of a high ridge of mountains, running obliquely acrofs the country for several hundred miles. It is very arid, except in some vallies, where the Dutch peasants have their habitations; but the general face of the country is rock. The soil is a red ochrey loam; it binds very hard in summer, and is in most places salt, which causes bad water. There is not a tree in the whole country, unless we should so call a few miserable shrubs, and of these the largest not exceeding two feet in height. The air is very sharp, and in winter they have frost and snow for several months, which obliges the Boors to remove, with all their flocks and herds, down to the Carro, or lower desarts, where they spend the winter; and at that time have plenty of fresh water, and all the shrubs green, which afford food for their cattle. They remove down in the beginning of May, when they have sown their corn, and return about the latter end of October, when the low country becomes parched, and the water turns salt, or is entirely dried up. All the game and ferocious animals observe the same removes.    The ancient inhabitants of this country, called by the Dutch Boschmenschen, are a savage people and very thievish; often carrying off 700 sheep at a time, and killing their shepherds. They use bows and arrows, and poison the arrows with the venom of serpents mixed with the juice of a species of *euphorbia*, which we had no opportunity of seeing. These Hottentots have neither flocks or herds, nor any fixed habitation, nor even skins to cover them; but live in the cavities of rocks, like baboons. Their common food is roots of plants, many of which we have not been able to discover. They eat snakes, lizards, scorpions, and all kind of reptiles.    There is a caterpillar which produces a very large moth, and is found commonly on the *mimosa nilotica.* These are found in great plenty, often stripping the trees of all their leaves, and of them the Hottentots make many a delicious meal. They also eat the

eggs

eggs of a large fpecies of ant, which they dig out of the ground in great quantities, wafhing them in water, and afterwards boiling them. They are commonly called Hottentot's rice. This is an excellent country for fheep; but the inhabitants breed few oxen, and thofe only for their own ufe. We found few plants here; but thofe we found were all new. I did not fee an *erica* or *protea* in the whole country.

22d, The ground was white with froft, and the wind fharp. At firft we propofed to continue our journey along the top of thefe mountains to the N.E. extremity; but our waggons were fo fhaken by the ruggednefs of the road, and our horfes and oxen fo tender-footed, that they became unferviceable, and we were obliged to drive them loofe a great part of the way home.

Dec. 2d, We thought of defcending the mountain, and directing our courfe to the Cape; but it blew a violent ftorm, and was extremely cold. The next morning the ground was white with froft, and there was ice upon the pools as thick as a crown piece. This alarmed the peafants, their wheat being then in bloffom, which they expected would be entirely deftroyed: a circumftance that often happens in this country.

3d, We were furnifhed with frefh oxen, and feveral Hottentots, who, with long thongs of leather fixed to the upper part of our waggons, kept them from overturning, while we were obliged to make both the hind

wheels

wheels faft with an iron chain to retard their motion.    After two hours and a half employed in hard labour, fometimes pulling on one fide, fometimes on the other, and fometimes all obliged to hang on with our whole ftrength behind the waggon, to keep it from running over the oxen, we arrived at the foot of the mountain, where we found the heat more troublefome than the cold had been on the top.    We now entered a large divifion of the Carro which lies along the foot of the Rogge Veld's Mountains, being a defart of four days journey, with no more than three pits of brackifh water to be found in all that extent, which was at this feafon forfaken by every living creature; but in winter it is the habitation of the Rogge Veld Boors, as I obferved before.

5th, To Unlucky River, called fo from a man having been there formerly devoured by a lion.  We remained here a day to reft our oxen, having found a pit with brackifh water, and fome reeds, which the oxen devoured with greedinefs.

8th, About eleven o'clock at night we got clear of the defart, and arrived at the foot of the Bocke Velde mountains, where we lodged by a rivulet of pure frefh water; and we fpent the remainder of that night and part of next day in great luxury.

11th, To Verkeerde Valley, where we refted three days, having found good pafture for our oxen, and a large lake of frefh water, well ftocked with water-fowl.  We
lived

lived on wild ducks and fnipes, though the fields abounded alfo with korhaans (a kind of buftard), partridges, hares, &c. and great flocks of oftriches.

15th, To Hexen Rivier, which runs along a narrow paffage through the great chain of mountains, between Rood Land and Zwellendam.    This valley is inclofed on each fide with impaffable mountains, whofe tops were ftill covered with fnow. There are feveral very genteel habitations in it, where we got fome wine and excellent fruit. We found many rare plants on the fides of thefe lofty mountains; and, I believe, there ftill remain many more entirely unknown to us.

18th, To Breede Rivier (Broad River).

22d, To Rood Land.

26th, To Paarde Berg.

28th, To the Cape Town.

M E T E-

www.ingramcontent.com/pod-product-compliance
Lightning Source LLC
Chambersburg PA
CBHW031811090426
42739CB00008B/1246